NO ONE REALLY KNOWS AN...

AXOLOTL

To my brother, Huw — the original sax-olotl — L.S.
For Violet Nymphadora — K.A.

Published in the UK by Scholastic, 2024
1 London Bridge, London, SE1 9BG
Scholastic Ireland, 89E Lagan Road, Dublin Industrial Estate, Glasnevin, Dublin, D11 HPSF

SCHOLASTIC and associated logos are trademarks and/or
registered trademarks of Scholastic Inc.

First published in Australia by Scholastic Australia, 2023

Text © Laura Sieveking, 2023
Illustrations © Katie Abey, 2023

The right of Laura Sieveking and Katie Abey to be identified
as the author and illustrator of this work has been asserted
by them under the Copyright, Designs and Patents Act 1988.

ISBN 978 0702 33766 6

A CIP catalogue record for this book is available from the British Library.

Printed in China
Paper made from wood grown in sustainable forests and other controlled sources.

10 9 8 7 6 5 4 3 2 1

www.scholastic.co.uk

NO ONE REALLY KNOWS AN...

AXOLOTL

Laura Sieveking   Katie Abey

SCHOLASTIC

Axolotl

Ear wax-olotl

Hiking trail backpacks-olotl

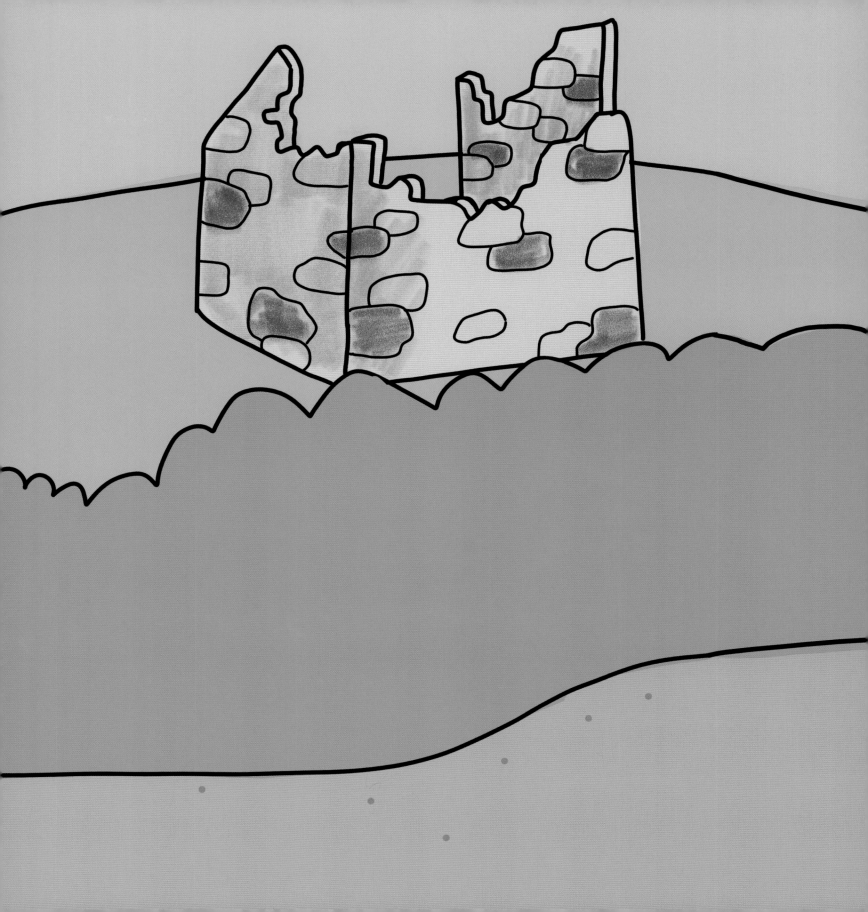

Fax-olotl

Snacks-olotl

Groovy jazzy sax-olotl

Max-olotl

Tracks-olotl

Riding a
humpbacks-olotl

Packs-olotl

Subtracts-olotl

Throwbacks-olotl

Wise-cracks-olotl

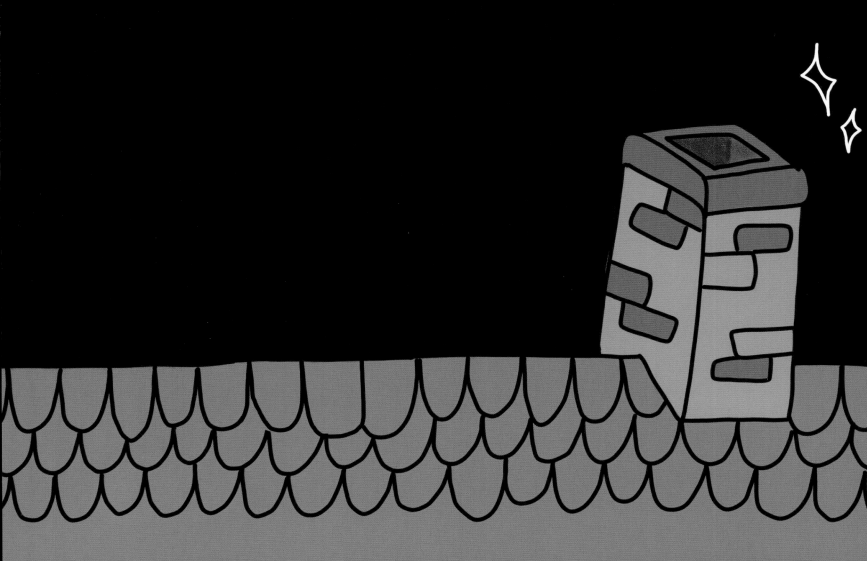

Quacks-olotl

Pickaxe-olotl

Slipping through the cracks-olotl

Hijacks-olotl

Nick-nacks-olotl

Time to go relax-olotl